ARCHAEOLOGY IN THE CITY

ARCHAEOLOGY IN THE CITY

A HOHOKAM VILLAGE IN PHOENIX, ARIZONA

Michael H. Bartlett, Thomas M. Kolaz, and David A. Gregory

UNIVERSITY OF ARIZONA PRESS, TUCSON

THE UNIVERSITY OF ARIZONA PRESS

Copyright ©1986 The Arizona Board of Regents, All Rights Reserved
Manufactured in the U.S.A.
This book was set in 10/12 I.T.C. Century Book Condensed

Library of Congress Cataloging-in-Publication Data

Bartlett, Michael H.
Archaeology in the city.
Bibliography: p.
1. Las Colinas Site (Phoenix, Ariz.)   2. Hohokam culture.   3. Phoenix (Ariz.)—Antiquities.
4. Excavations (Archaeology)—Arizona.   5. Arizona—Antiquities. I. Kolaz, Thomas M.
II. Gregory, David A.   III. Title. E99.H68B37   1986   979.1'73   86-918
ISBN 0-8165-0970-0 (alk. paper)

If people are to be led to
feel themselves members of
a world society, one way to
help them to do so is
to stimulate a conscious-
ness of world history.
Prehistory ... finds complete
justification if it enriches
the experience of men and
helps them to live more
abundantly as heirs of all
ages and brothers to one
another.

Grahame Clark

ACKNOWLEDGMENTS

The authors would like to extend their sincere appreciation to David A. Phillips, Jr., Raymond H. Thompson, and Carol Ann Heathington for their substantial contributions to the development of this book. Our thanks also to the Special Collections Division of the University of Arizona Library for the use of the map reproduced on page 26 and to the Arizona State Museum for permission to use the photographs printed herein. Drafted maps and line drawings are the work of Charles S. Sternberg and Ronald Beckwith.

This volume has been prepared with the support of the Arizona Department of Transportation in cooperation with the Federal Highways Administration.

TABLE OF CONTENTS

1. Introduction 13

2. The Desert People 17

3. The Hohokam Village of Las Colinas 37

4. A Complex Wealth of Information 55

5. Archaeology and the Public 65

Suggested Readings 71

The study of man and civilization is not only a matter of scientific interest, but at once it passes into the practical business of life. We have in it the means of understanding our own lives and our own place in the world…more clearly than any former generation. The knowledge of man's course of life, from the remote past to the present, will guide us in our duty of leaving the world better than we found it.

E. B. Tyler

CHAPTER ONE

INTRODUCTION

Within the next few years, thousands of motorists will enter the city of Phoenix from the west on Interstate Highway 10. As they approach downtown Phoenix, few of these travelers will know that they are passing over the site of an ancient Hohokam Indian village called Las Colinas. The Hohokam were a prehistoric people who lived in southern Arizona, and Las Colinas was one of the largest of the Hohokam villages. Many of these villages now lie beneath metropolitan Phoenix, covered by the streets, houses, and businesses of that sprawling city. Many archaeological sites have been disturbed or destroyed by modern development, but much is preserved and our knowledge of the people who lived in this area hundreds of years ago can be considerably increased by studying those remains.

During 1982, 1983, and 1984, archaeologists from the Arizona State Museum at the University of Arizona excavated parts of Las Colinas that were to be

Beneath the Phoenix skyline, in the path of Interstate 10, the remains of the Hohokam village of Las Colinas are unearthed. Lines of chalk in the center of the photograph mark the course of the small canal which formed the western edge of the village. The open area of the excavations in progress may be seen to the east of the canal, along with large piles of back dirt produced by the excavations. The two areas outlined in the foreground were settling basins where the villagers collected clay, probably for making pottery.

ARCHAEOLOGY IN THE CITY

affected by the construction of Interstate 10. This research, sponsored by the Arizona Department of Transportation in cooperation with the Federal Highways Administration, was accomplished in accordance with the federal and state laws that govern and protect our nation's cultural resources. By sponsoring the research at Las Colinas, these agencies insured that valuable scientific information contained in these sites would be properly collected, analyzed, and, in that way, preserved. For over fourteen months, archaeological crews labored painstakingly, uncovering the remains of the prehistoric village, recording in minute detail the information slowly yielded by the site. After the excavation, over two years of laboratory work began. The maps and drawings made in the field and the pieces of broken pottery, stone tools, and other artifacts collected there were closely examined for answers to the questions posed by the archaeologists: How many people lived in the village? When did they live there? What did they eat? Were there leaders with special status in the community? How did their society change and grow during the life of the village? These and many other questions have been addressed, and further refinement of our knowledge of the Hohokam will result from the research that continues even as this book is being written.

The Las Colinas project is one of many endeavors currently expanding our knowledge of the Hohokam in the Salt River Valley. Archaeologists from Arizona State University recently excavated a Hohokam site called La Ciudad, which also lay in the path of the new Interstate 10 freeway. In recent years, federal, state, and local governmental agencies, as well as commercial developers, have sponsored similar projects throughout the Phoenix Basin. This research has added substantially to our understanding of the prehistory of the area. Although not all projects are as large as the one undertaken at Las Colinas, each contributes new information and insights.

The skyline of downtown Phoenix is not the kind of setting usually associated with archaeology. The mystery and excitement of the far away and exotic are more commonly held images, fostered by exhibits of priceless archaeological treasures, such as relics from Tutankhamen's tomb, and reinforced by motion pictures in the romantic adventure tradition. The truth is that the conduct of archaeology requires long and difficult physical labor, hours of meticulous and

14

INTRODUCTION

sometimes tedious study, and the slow and careful evaluation of thousands of time-worn artifacts. And, as the excavations at Las Colinas well illustrate, archaeology is not always practiced in exotic locations.

Yet there is mystery and excitement of a different and more lasting kind. The treasures at Las Colinas are not gold and silver or priceless artifacts, but information about the lifeways of the people who lived so long ago in the Arizona desert. To excavate and interpret an archaeological site is to come into contact with the people who created it, to understand something of how they lived their lives and, indirectly, how they arranged and thought about their world. Despite a decidedly unromantic setting within urban Phoenix, the excavations at Las Colinas produced a sense of wonder and discovery in both the professionals who worked at the site and the members of the general public who came to view the work in progress. In the pages that follow, the reader will learn something of the Hohokam, of the prehistoric village of Las Colinas, of the work of modern archaeologists, and of the importance of archaeology to the general public. By providing a brief glimpse of a portion of Arizona's past and of the ways in which that past is studied, this book is a way to share the very real emotions of excitement, wonder, and discovery that archaeology can produce in all of us.

The Hohokam were not one of the world's great societies, but they revealed a strain of greatness characterized by a cultural form or style that insured unusual stability. By placing primacy on the earth and by being protective of their environment, they forged a social and economic system that enjoyed 1,500 years of ascendency.

My view of Hohokam success, epitomized by their long history, is that they effectively blended their technical know-how with the resources of nature available to them.

Emil W. Haury

CHAPTER TWO

THE
DESERT PEOPLE

The word "desert" often conjures up an image of a dry and desolate wasteland, devoid of life and scoured by blowing sand. In some desert environments of the world, this image is at least partly correct. In the Sonoran Desert regions of southern Arizona, however, such a picture is erroneous. Though hot and dry, the desert valleys support an abundant plant and animal life that can provide more than adequate sustenance for those who know how to use the available resources. The Hohokam were such a people.

The origins of the Hohokam are still a matter of debate among archaeologists. Some believe that Hohokam society developed out of earlier groups known as Southwestern Archaic cultures (7000 B.C. to about 300 B.C.). These people were hunters and gatherers who lived a nomadic existence, moving around the desert in small groups, taking advantage of natural cycles of plant and animal availability and abundance. In this view, the introduction of corn from Mexico resulted in changes in this lifeway, as an increasing dependence on corn and other cultivated plants caused the people to move around less and less frequently, and eventually to become settled farmers. Because of similarities between pottery and other artifacts found in Hohokam sites and those found in archaeological sites far to the south, other archaeologists believe that the Hohokam represent a group of people who migrated from an as yet unidentified location in Mexico. They brought with them their knowledge of agriculture and canal irrigation, as well as other traits, to introduce a completely new way of life to the desert river valleys. Still others think that both of these ideas are true: groups migrating from Mexico found people already living in the deserts and merged with them to produce the distinctive Hohokam culture.

Whatever their origins may have been, the Hohokam quickly forged a successful adjustment to desert living, ultimately occupying much of what is today known as southern Arizona. By diverting the waters of the Salt and Gila rivers onto their fields, they produced crops which, when supplemented by wild plant and animal resources, provided a stable food supply for a growing population. Thus, the Hohokam laid the foundation for a culture that was to endure for many centuries.

Other major prehistoric Southwestern cultural groups identified by archaeologists are the Mogollon, the Anasazi, and the Patayan (see map). The Mogollon occupied the mountainous areas and the basins and ranges of central Arizona and west-central New Mexico, while the Anasazi lived in the canyons and valleys of the Colorado Plateau and the Four Corners area of Arizona, New Mexico, Colorado, and Utah. Patayan peoples occupied much of northwestern Arizona and the valley of the Colorado River. Like the Hohokam, each of these groups had their own distinctive ways of building dwellings, making pottery and other craft items, and treating the dead, as well as different modes of subsistence which set them off from one another. They probably held different religious beliefs and spoke different languages as well.

Among the characteristics that distinguish the Hohokam from other prehistoric groups in the American Southwest are a settled village way of life, a canal irrigation technology, a distinctive red-on-buff pottery, an elaborate craftwork in marine shell, the practice of cremating the dead, the manufacture of clay figurines, and the construction and use of ballcourts and platform mounds. Archaeologists have traced the basic outline of Hohokam prehistory and have divided it into large blocks of time called periods; these are further

---

Beautiful and distinctive items made by the prehistoric Hohokam. Red-on-buff pottery, clay figurines, elaborate shell ornaments, and flaked and ground stone tools are hallmarks of their culture.

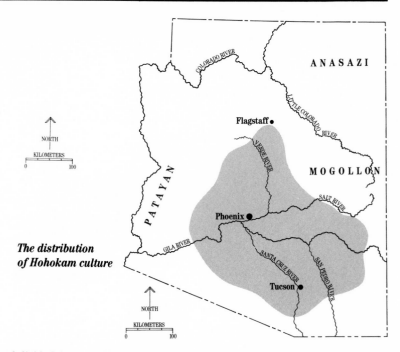

The distribution of Hohokam culture

subdivided into smaller units called phases (see chart). These divisions are based on the changes which occurred in pottery, house form, and other elements of material culture during the Hohokam tenure in the desert.

The lives of the Hohokam centered on the activities that took place in the villages. It was there that people built their houses and lived most of the year. Food was brought there from the fields for processing and storage, and it was in the village that pottery and other necessary tools were manufactured. Religious activities were a part of village life as well, and people who had died were cremated and buried there. Many village activities probably revolved around family groups or sets of families related by marriage who lived and worked together.

In the villages and smaller settlements, the people built and lived in houses well suited to the desert environment. The principal form of dwelling built by

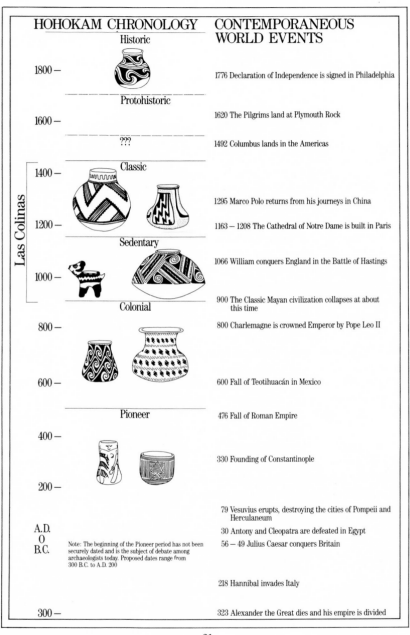

HOHOKAM CHRONOLOGY

CONTEMPORANEOUS WORLD EVENTS

Historic

1800 —

1776 Declaration of Independence is signed in Philadelphia

Protohistoric

1600 —

1620 The Pilgrims land at Plymouth Rock

???

1492 Columbus lands in the Americas

Classic

1400 —

Las Colinas

1295 Marco Polo returns from his journeys in China

1200 —

1163 — 1208 The Cathedral of Notre Dame is built in Paris

Sedentary

1066 William conquers England in the Battle of Hastings

1000 —

900 The Classic Mayan civilization collapses at about this time

Colonial

800 —

800 Charlemagne is crowned Emperor by Pope Leo II

600 —

600 Fall of Teotihuacán in Mexico

Pioneer

476 Fall of Roman Empire

400 —

330 Founding of Constantinople

200 —

79 Vesuvius erupts, destroying the cities of Pompeii and Herculaneum

A.D.

30 Antony and Cleopatra are defeated in Egypt

0

56 — 49 Julius Caesar conquers Britain

B.C.

Note: The beginning of the Pioneer period has not been securely dated and is the subject of debate among archaeologists today. Proposed dates range from 300 B.C. to A.D. 200

218 Hannibal invades Italy

300 —

323 Alexander the Great dies and his empire is divided

the Hohokam during most of their history was the pit house (see below). In the construction of these houses, an elongate oval-shaped or subrectangular pit was first dug into the ground, to a depth of approximately 1 foot. A superstructure was created by placing posts of mesquite or other desert wood upright at intervals around the margins of the pit to frame the walls; posts within these walls supported the roof. Additional posts were placed across these uprights, and sticks and brush were added to fill in the larger spaces, probably creating a structure with a rounded roof. On top of this a layer of grasses and reeds was added and often covered with mud. The floors of most houses were plastered with a caliche-rich mud, giving them a distinctive whitish color. Nearly every house floor included a bowl-shaped hearth, located just inside the doorway and nicely finished with a coating of plaster. Entryways were almost always centered in one side of the long axis of the house. This combination of materials, along with the sunken floor, caused the structures to retain heat in winter and to be relatively cool during the hot desert summer. Because rainfall was infrequent, the mud covering did not deteriorate as quickly as it would have done in a wetter environment. Still, it was necessary to refurbish, repair, or rebuild the houses periodically; termites or infestations of other insects often caused the destruction or abandonment of houses, and

Hohokam house construction: pit house

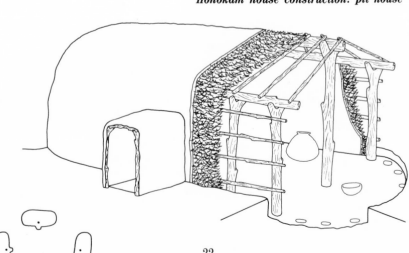

fires destroyed others. Some fires were accidental, but houses may have been intentionally burned upon the death of one of the occupants.

During the Classic period, other house forms were developed. Many Classic period houses were not dug so deeply into the ground as the earlier houses (some not at all), had square corners and a fully rectangular or square shape, and probably had flatter roofs than the pit houses (see below). The walls of some were constructed in essentially the same way as those of the earlier style—a post, stick, and brush frame covered with mud—but a new technique for constructing walls without posts was also developed. This method resulted in what is called *coursed adobe* architecture; it was accomplished by simply piling up wet, caliche-rich adobe, allowing it to dry, piling on more wet adobe, and so on, until the wall reached the desired height. The beams that supported the roofs of such houses rested directly on the walls, and the sticks, brush, and mud that made up the roof were placed on top of the beams. These new kinds of rooms were in many cases combined into apartmentlike constructions, with sets of contiguous rooms often grouped inside an enclosing wall or compound. Thus, during the Classic period there were changes not only in the kinds of structures built but also in the manner in which they were grouped together.

and coursed-adobe structure

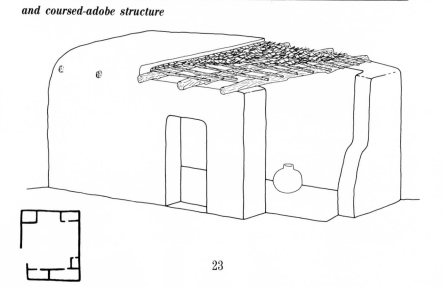

23

ARCHAEOLOGY IN THE CITY

Although house shapes and details of construction changed over time, the basic conception and construction of the Hohokam house was consistent for many centuries, and even in the Classic period, when new architectural forms were used, pit houses continued to be built.

In the houses, the people slept, cooked, or warmed their meals, stored surplus food, and manufactured some of the tools and ornaments that are found in archaeological sites today. Some houses were probably used only for the storage of foodstuffs, rather than being places where people actually lived. Most houses were relatively small and were probably lit only by sunlight coming through the doorway. Throughout the village we find evidence of activities that required more light and space than was available inside the houses. Large pits full of charcoal, ash, and fire-cracked rock where plant foods were roasted, basins in which potter's clay was mixed, as well as other extramural features, indicate that many tasks were performed outside.

Many of the everyday tasks performed in the village involved the use or manufacture of utilitarian tools—the pots and pans of Hohokam culture. Among the most important of these were the metate and mano, the hard stone implements with which corn was ground into flour. The kinds of stone suitable for the manufacture of metates and manos often had to be transported to the village from miles away, and these artifacts were probably valued personal items among the women of the villages—perhaps they were even passed down from mother to daughter. A great variety of ceramic vessels was also manufactured for use in everyday activities: jars for carrying and storing water and for cooking; bowls for serving; and scoops for getting food or water out of the larger pots. Axes for felling trees and chopping wood were laboriously pecked and ground to shape from hard igneous rocks. Chipped stone tools—sharp points for arrows and knives which served a variety of purposes—were made of locally available stone. The broken pieces of these common tools are the most abundant artifacts recovered from Hohokam sites. Undoubtedly, they also fashioned many items for everyday use out of perishable materials that are only rarely recovered from archaeological sites. Basketry containers made from grasses and the stems of woody plants were probably used for a variety of different purposes, and such important tools as the digging sticks

THE DESERT PEOPLE

used to cultivate the fields and the handles for stone axes were made of wood.

It was also in and around the houses in the village that specialized shell, stone, and bone artifacts were manufactured. Marine shell, obtained from the Gulf of California and from the Pacific coast of California, was made into a wide variety of pendants, bracelets, rings, and other items of adornment. Much of the shell was cut with stone tools, then ground and polished, but the Hohokam also developed the technique of *etching* to decorate the surface of some pieces. This was accomplished by first outlining a design on the surface of the shell and covering it with pitch. The shell was then immersed in a weak acid solution, probably made from the juices of cactus fruit, and left until the acid had partly eaten away the unprotected areas on the shell's surface, leaving a raised design. Nowhere else in the world has this technique ever been used to decorate shell; it is a unique Hohokam invention and an important aspect of their distinctive shell-working industry.

The Hohokam also carved bowls, beads, pendants, and other ornaments out of a number of different kinds of soft stone. Most favored was argillite, a metamorphic rock with a deep maroon red color, which comes from deposits in the middle reaches of the Verde River, in central Arizona. Although many Hohokam stone carvings are simple, one-dimensional figures, some of them are quite elaborate, and the outside surfaces of stone bowls are often carved with full-relief human or animal figures. Bone was also carved into ornaments such as rings and hair pins, and some of these carved artifacts were also painted.

The shell and stone worked by Hohokam craftsmen were probably acquired both from trade with other Hohokam and non-Hohokam people and through expeditions mounted specifically for the purpose of obtaining these materials. It may also be that such skilled crafts were not practiced in every Hohokam village but that the people of smaller communities obtained these items from artisans in the larger settlements.

Not all Hohokam people lived in the villages for the entire year; some groups probably moved near the fields during the growing season to tend the crops and to do the work of diverting water from the canals onto the fields at the

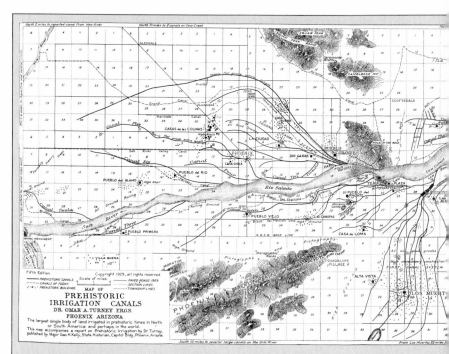

Canals: Lifeblood of the River Villages

This early map of the Hohokam canals on the north side of the Salt River was made by Omar Turney, an engineer who took a great interest in the accomplishments of the Hohokam.

One of the most impressive accomplishments of the Hohokam was the construction of extensive canal systems, which diverted water from rivers to fields and villages up to 6 miles away from the river channels. The Hohokam canals represent the most complex and extensive water control system that existed in

prehistoric North America north of Mexico. Canals were built along the Salt, Gila, and Verde rivers, but the most complex canal systems were those on the Salt, in the fertile valley now occupied by urban Phoenix.

The village of Las Colinas, located some 3 miles from the Salt River, was made possible in part by the canals that brought water into the area.

A small canal at Las Colinas. The size of Hohokam canals ranged from over 20 meters (about 64 feet) wide to canals of the size shown here, less than 2 meters (about 6 feet) wide. From the large canals that took water directly off the river, the water was diverted into ever smaller channels, finally reaching the fields to irrigate the growing crops. The canals also provided water for drinking, cooking, pottery making, and other everyday uses.

appropriate times. Other families probably lived permanently in smaller settlements away from the rivers in locations where rainfall and other naturally available moisture were sufficient to produce small crops, or where the abundance of wild foods was great. Most of the Hohokam population, however, was concentrated along the rivers, and it was here that large villages like Las Colinas developed. The practice of canal irrigation permitted this concentration, by supporting cultivation of a much greater area of land than would have been possible if the Hohokam had depended only on the infrequent desert rains (see box, pages 26 and 27).

In their irrigated fields, the people grew a variety of crops. Beans, squash, and cotton were produced, in addition to the ever-important corn, and a variety of wild plant foods were also exploited. The seed pods of mesquite and screwbean trees were ground into flour, fruit from several varieties of cacti were eaten and probably fermented into an alcoholic beverage, the hearts of agave plants were roasted and eaten, and the seeds of many plants we think of today as weeds were ground and used in stews and gruels. Meat probably did not play a major role in the Hohokam diet, but small animals such as rabbits were hunted and eaten, and occasionally a larger animal such as a deer or antelope was added to the stew pot. Food for immediate consumption was cooked by roasting or boiling or was eaten raw. Food to be stored for future use was roasted, parched, or simply air-dried, and then protected until it was needed by being stored in baskets, pottery vessels, or pits dug into the earth. Cotton seeds were probably eaten, and cotton fiber was spun into thread and used to weave cloth for garments.

Although we know little of Hohokam religion, many of their concerns with the supernatural must have revolved around the power to influence the productivity of both cultivated and natural resources, and around the trauma of death. Both concerns often play important roles in the belief systems or religions of preliterate agricultural peoples, and were probably also important to the prehistoric Hohokam. Community ritual activities may have centered on the ballcourts—large elliptical depressions surrounded by earthen embankments—found in most villages, where some version of the Mesoamerican ball game may have been played (see box, page 29). In prehistoric Mexico, the ball

Ballcourts

Hohokam ballcourts are large, oval depressions excavated into the ground and surrounded by earthen embankments. Stones were often set into the floors of the courts, at the center, and at both ends, perhaps to serve as markers in the game played there. The interior surfaces of the courts were usually smoothly plastered; this characteristic, as well as the volume of earth moved, suggests that a great deal of work went into their construction. As may be seen in the photographs below, Hohokam ballcourts vary greatly in size, from the very large court at the village of Snaketown, which covers an area the size of a modern football field, to very small courts such as the one discovered at Las Colinas. Nearly every village had one of these courts, and some had two or more, probably reflecting the social and religious importance of the settlement.

Comparisons with similar structures found in archaeological sites in Mexico suggest that a version of the rubber-ball game played there may have been known to the Hohokam. It is believed that among the Hohokam, as in Mexico, the game was more than a sport. It was probably the focus of a ritual performance that embodied cultural beliefs and served to bring together people from various communities.

The large ballcourt at Snaketown

The ballcourt at Las Colinas

ARCHAEOLOGY IN THE CITY

bouncing between the players on opposing teams represented the sun struggling to rise out of the night sky and then falling again at the end of the day, as well as the changing of the seasons. A similar belief may have been held by the Hohokam and dramatized by them in the ballcourts. During the Classic period, the focus of village rituals may have shifted from the ballcourts to the platform mounds, another form of public architecture constructed by the Hohokam. In addition to the rituals that took place in the ballcourts and on the mounds, other important ceremonies probably accompanied the cremation and burial of the dead.

Over the centuries, the Hohokam populations grew, old villages were enlarged, new villages were established, and new lands were brought under cultivation by the expansion of the canal systems. Although variations of the basic Hohokam pattern—such as minor differences in pottery and other artifacts and the degree of dependence on irrigation agriculture—developed in different areas, this distinctive lifeway had spread across much of southern and central Arizona by the Colonial period. Relationships were established and maintained with the Anasazi, Mogollon, and Patayan peoples who lived outside the desert valleys, attested to by the foreign pottery and marine shell found in Hohokam sites.

Sometime around A.D. 1100, in the latter part of the Sedentary period, changes began to occur within Hohokam society. While the people still lived in their villages and irrigated their fields, the changes in the construction and arrangement of houses mentioned above, as well as shifts in many aspects of the material culture signaled basic alterations in the Hohokam way of life. The typical red-on-buff pottery began to decline in popularity, to be replaced by a red ware pottery without painted designs, and, later, by a polychrome ware having black and white designs on a red background. Fewer ballcourts were constructed, and some of the old ones were abandoned, perhaps indicating a change in the religious outlook of the people. As noted above, a new architectural form—the platform mound—appeared; these impressive features, built only in the larger villages, required substantial time and labor for their construction (see box, pages 32 and 33).

THE DESERT PEOPLE

Several ideas have been put forward to explain these changes. Some archaeologists believe that the Salado, a Mogollon people from central Arizona, migrated to the Hohokam area and that the observed changes are the result of the blending of the Hohokam culture with that of the northern people. Others believe that the establishment of ties with highly organized groups in Mexico had something to do with the alteration of Hohokam society. Still others think that these changes were not the result of external influences but were caused by the development within Hohokam society of groups of individuals having elite status, people who exercised great control over the lives and actions of most of the villagers.

Although an interpretation of the changes that mark the Classic period has not been agreed upon, the excavations at Las Colinas provided an ideal opportunity to examine in detail this important period. Studies of the Las Colinas material indicate that the changes probably resulted primarily from the action of forces within Hohokam society, not from without, and that the development of elite groups or at least a greater degree of social differentiation within the society may have caused some of the observed shifts. The material from Las Colinas also suggests that the changes may have been more gradual than was previously thought.

By approximately A.D. 1450, and possibly somewhat earlier, the Hohokam villages had been largely abandoned. Although there are some indications that small groups of people remained in the area for an unknown period after this date, it is clear that the population had been drastically reduced and that the villages were no longer the scene of the myriad activities that had once taken place there. The canal systems ceased to function, and the once productive fields were left to be taken over once more by the desert. By the time the first Spanish explorers arrived in the area, the villages had been in ruins for two hundred years and the Hohokam were the subject of legends told by the indigenous peoples of the region—the Pima and Papago.

As is the case with Hohokam origins and the changes that occurred at the end of the Sedentary period, there is debate among archaeologists as to the reasons for the Hohokam decline and its ultimate results. It was once thought

Platform Mounds

One of the hallmarks of the Classic period is the appearance of a new architectural form: the platform mound. These features are artificially constructed elevations with flat tops. The earliest platform mounds were small, round constructions measuring only 10 m (about 33 ft.) across and less than 1 m (about 3.3 ft.) high; they were surrounded by a palisade of upright posts that may have supported a brush covering.

As this form of architecture developed, the mounds became larger and were constructed by a different technique. First, a wall was built outlining the shape of the mound, and the space within the wall was filled with trash, desert soil, or both. The top of the mound was then covered with a plastered surface. Sometimes a small structure, like the pit houses found in the villages, was built on top of the mound. Some of the mounds eventually grew to be quite large, measuring as much as 60 m (about 198 ft.) on a side and over 8 m (about 26 ft.) in height. All of them were surrounded by a solid wall, a feature which probably developed out of the earlier palisade.

The probability that the mounds were used for ritual activities in which only part of the community participated is indicated by the limited space on the top of the mounds and within the walls which surrounded them. The walls formed a physical barrier separating the mound precinct from the rest of the village; in addition to restricting access to the area, they may also have reduced the visibility of the activities that went on there.

At some time during their development—probably around A.D. 1250—the way in which the platform mounds were used apparently changed. Instead of a single small structure, whole complexes of rooms were built on the mounds, indicating that, for the first time, groups of people were actually living there.

The distribution of platform mounds is much more restricted than that of ballcourts; with few exceptions, they were built only at the major villages along the canals on the Salt and Gila rivers. Most sites had only one platform mound, but some sites had two and, very rarely, more. As with the ballcourts, the presence, size, and number of these mounds may reflect the social and religious importance of the community. The decline in the construction and use of ballcourts and the development and spread of platform mounds occurred at about the same time, perhaps reflecting changes in the focus, and possibly the nature, of Hohokam ritual activity. The fact that groups of people began to live on the mounds may be evidence that differences in status had developed within Hohokam society, with the individuals or families of high status dwelling on the mounds.

Much remains to be learned about these impressive features and their place in Hohokam society; unfortunately, many of them have now been destroyed. There were originally at least four platform mounds at Las Colinas, one of which was explored in 1968 and again during the recent excavations at the site (see Chapter 3). The excavation of this mound provided a wealth of new information concerning the architectural development and function of Hohokam platform mounds.

A later platform mound at Escalante, another site along the Gila River

An early platform mound at Snaketown

Helga Teiwes

that the incursions of marauding Apaches from the north and east caused the abandonment of the desert villages, but it has since been shown that the Apaches did not arrive in Arizona until the 1600s, well after the Hohokam demise. Some scientists think that conflict within the society between the Hohokam and their new Salado neighbors caused the decline. Others believe that environmental change made it impossible for the Hohokam to use their extensive canal systems and that the remnants of a once-thriving Hohokam society migrated to the east and north, mingling with other groups, losing their Hohokam identity, and leaving the deserts without people. Still others think that these same environmental changes caused a reduction in population but that some people remained in the Arizona deserts and were found there when the Spanish explorers arrived. These peoples—the Pima and Papago Indians—are then the direct descendants of the Hohokam. There are many similarities between the culture of the Pima and Papago and that of the Hohokam, such as the form of houses and the means by which desert plants are cooked, preserved, and stored, but the available scientific evidence does not conclusively support one theory or the other. Among the modern Pima and Papago, however, there is no doubt: they believe strongly that the Hohokam were their ancestors.

The reason for the decline of Hohokam culture in the fifteenth century is only one of many questions that remain to be answered about the prehistoric desert dwellers. Our knowledge of the Hohokam has been gained only through years of work by many archaeologists, and many more years of dedicated study and research will be required to answer all of these questions. Although many of these important issues are as yet unresolved, we can marvel at the achievements of the prehistoric Hohokam. By combining their knowledge of the environment with diligent labor, these people lived successfully and even prosperously for over 1000 years, true masters of the desert.

The 29th I went by myself to visit another group of ruins located 3 miles to the west of town; the ruins here were much more extensive than those which I visited to the east of Phoenix; they consisted of several of those large terraced mounds already described, and of a ring in elliptical form which appeared to me to have served as a place of assembly or as a court for games.

Alphonse Pinart
January 1876

A modern sewer trench, with the pipe at the bottom, can be seen cutting through the Hohokam trash pit being excavated here. Much of Las Colinas survived such modern disturbances as plowing and house construction.

CHAPTER THREE

THE HOHOKAM VILLAGE OF LAS COLINAS

The brief description quoted on page 35 was recorded by the Frenchman Alphonse Pinart, who was one of the first trained observers to view the ruins of Las Colinas. In 1876, the site must have looked much as it had since the Hohokam abandoned it in the fifteenth century, with only the natural forces of wind and water and the growth of desert plants to erode and obscure the remains of the former community. Within five years of Pinart's visit, however, agricultural development of the Phoenix area began in earnest, and the places where Hohokam houses once stood soon became plowed fields where wheat and beets were grown. Between the late 1800s and the early 1930s, nearly all of the area of the former village was brought under cultivation, resulting in destruction and disturbance of the prehistoric remains. With the later westward expansion of metropolitan Phoenix, plowed fields gave way to streets, residential areas, and small businesses, and it became difficult to imagine that a large prehistoric community had once flourished there. Many other Hohokam sites in the Phoenix area suffered a similar fate, covered and obscured by twentieth-century development.

Fortunately, the growth of modern Phoenix also brought to the area men who developed a keen and abiding interest in the earlier occupants of the valley. Many saw the old canals and ruins that dotted the landscape and wondered about the people who had constructed them. Although few of these men were professional archaeologists, they made maps of the ruins and canals and took

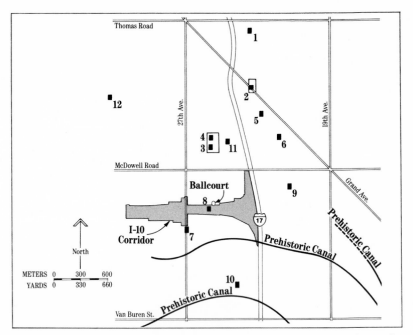

Frank Midvale's 1968 map of Las Colinas showing the twelve numbered mounds. The Interstate 10 corridor is indicated by shading.

notes and photographs that in some cases constitute the only information about the prehistoric villages that now survives. It was probably one of these men—the engineer Omar A. Turney—who named the site Las Colinas. Las Colinas means "the knolls" in Spanish and refers to the large number of mounds that were once visible there. Another individual who made outstanding contributions to the archaeology of the Phoenix area was Frank Midvale. Midvale did have some professional training as an archaeologist, and he knew the importance of documenting the prehistoric ruins to the fullest extent possible. His 1968 map of Las Colinas shows that the site once had twelve large mounds and a ballcourt, distributed across an area of over 1 square mile (see map above).

38

HOHOKAM VILLAGE OF LAS COLINAS

This photograph shows Mound 7 at Las Colinas as it appeared sometime prior to 1929. A dirt road, later 27th Avenue, cuts through the mound; the rest of the mound was later graded down. A similar fate was suffered by all the Las Colinas mounds except Mound 8.

A photograph of the house built on Mound 8 as it appeared in 1917. The long life of this modern house probably saved the ancient mound from destruction.

ARCHAEOLOGY IN THE CITY

By the late 1930s, all but one of the mounds that had given the site its name had been destroyed. Many of them were cut through by the roads of an expanding Phoenix (see the photograph, page 39), and some were actually dug up and hauled away for road fill. Still others were simply plowed under as more land was brought under cultivation. Only Mound 8 survived, the result of a fortunate turn of history.

In 1889, a farmhouse was built atop Mound 8 (see the photograph, page 39). The practice of constructing houses on prehistoric mounds was a common one during the early days of Phoenix, because these were the only hills in the otherwise flat terrain. Most of the houses were later abandoned and torn down along with the mounds, but the house on Mound 8 remained standing until 1956, when it burned. By this time, the city had expanded around the old farmhouse, and land values were not high enough to foster rapid development of the area. The mound became little more than a curiosity and a place where neighborhood children played.

When the Arizona Department of Transportation began to plan for the construction of the Interstate 10 freeway, it was recognized that Mound 8 lay directly in the path of the proposed highway. The Arizona State Museum was contacted, and plans for an excavation were made. From May through October of 1968, archaeologists under the direction of Laurens C. Hammack labored in the heat of a Phoenix summer, excavating large portions of the mound and collecting much information about its construction and history.

For the next ten years, plans for the freeway proceeded slowly. Alternative routes were considered, and public support for construction of the highway waxed and waned. The intervening years also saw the passage of federal legislation protecting cultural resources, and by the time the plans for the freeway were finalized, much stricter laws were in effect regarding the treatment of archaeological sites. In addition, Hammack's excavation had been largely restricted to the immediate area of the mound, since most of the land within the freeway corridor to the west had not been acquired by the state in 1968. No research had been conducted in areas away from the mound and little was known of the overall character of the village. New questions about the

The foundation of a house built in the 1950s overlies the floors of Hohokam houses of the eleventh and twelfth centuries A.D.

nature of Hohokam platform mounds and their role in the society had also been raised over the years. In 1980, it was apparent that additional studies would be required prior to the building of the highway. After a long process of testing those parts of the site outside the vicinity of Mound 8, and competitive bidding for the opportunity to do the additional work (in accordance with federal legislation), the Arizona State Museum was awarded a contract to perform the research. Archaeological investigations at Las Colinas began once again in October of 1982.

As the excavations proceeded, it became apparent that much of the site had survived the intrusions of the modern world. Despite historic plowing, residential development, and road construction, the remains of the Hohokam village were found to be remarkably well preserved. Beneath the modern disturbance, the complexities of the site began to reveal themselves to the trained eyes and skilled hands of the archaeologists (see the photograph, page 41).

By the time the excavations had been completed, over 2,000 individual features had been excavated. The remains of numerous houses, several canals, a ballcourt, storage pits, roasting pits, cremations, and various other features were uncovered. Nearly a million artifacts were recovered, and thousands of samples were collected. These samples included soil taken from the fill of pits and scraped from the floors of houses, which would be examined in the laboratory for pollen grains, tiny seeds, pieces of wood and plant fibers, bone fragments, and other evidence of the plants and animals used by the villagers. Other samples were taken for chronometric analyses which would indicate the age of the site (see box, pages 44-47). Pages upon pages of notes were written and hundreds of drawings and photographs made, to record and preserve information about each excavated feature for later study and analysis.

The size and complexity of the site are shown on the map of the major features uncovered at Las Colinas on the following page. The excavations were confined to the proposed freeway corridor and represent only a small fraction of this major prehistoric village; nonetheless, the excavations provided a better understanding of the size and organization of the village and of the changes that occurred there during the occupation. The kinds of pottery

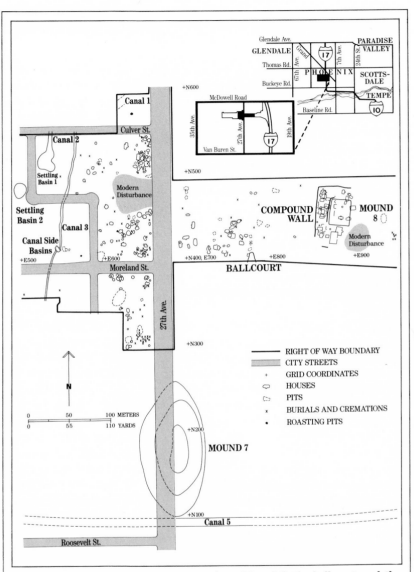

Map of Las Colinas after recent excavations. Mound 8, the ballcourt, and the many houses that made up the village may be seen along with the canal that formed the western boundary of the village.

How Old Is the Village?

One of the most important tasks of the archaeologist is determining the age of the materials recovered from sites and of the sites themselves. Chemists, physicists, and archaeologists have worked together to develop a variety of techniques for dating. One such method is *radiocarbon dating*, which employs specimens of once-living matter, such as pieces of charcoal or undecayed wood recovered from sites. All living things contain radioactive isotopes of carbon which begin to decay at a fixed rate upon the death of the plant or animal. By measuring the amounts of the different isotopes, it is possible to determine how long the decay has been going on and thus the age of the specimen. Another chronometric method is *dendrochronology*, or tree-ring dating. By matching series of rings from certain species of living pine trees with pieces of similar wood from archaeological sites, scientists have been able to reconstruct a long series of rings whose characteristics are known. By matching the characteristics of wood taken from sites with the known series, the age of the archaeological specimen can be determined, sometimes to the year the tree was cut.

Both of these methods have their shortcomings. The dates obtained by radiocarbon dating are sometimes not precise enough to be useful in the interpretation of Hohokam sites. The species of pine used for dendrochronology do not grow in the desert, and only rarely are the right kinds of wood recovered from Hohokam sites.

A relatively new method, called *archaeomagnetic dating*, has been developed over the last two decades and provides a means by which the remains of these desert dwellers may be placed in time. The magnetic north pole is not stationary; its geographic position changes constantly. Scientists have charted some of its wanderings (see page 45), so that its position at various times in the past is known. Many soils and clays contain iron particles—mostly magnetites and hematites—which, under certain conditions, become aligned with the earth's magnetic field, reflecting the location of the magnetic pole at that time. If they become fixed in that position and are not subsequently disturbed, the age of this event may be determined by archaeomagnetic dating.

The clays with which the Hohokam built and lined the hearths in their houses contained such particles. The heat from the fire in the hearth caused them to align with the earth's magnetic field. As the clay cooled, the particles were frozen in this position, pointing like a compass toward the position of the north pole *at that time*. By taking samples from the Hohokam hearths, measuring the direction in which the magnetic particles point, and matching that direction to known pole positions, it is

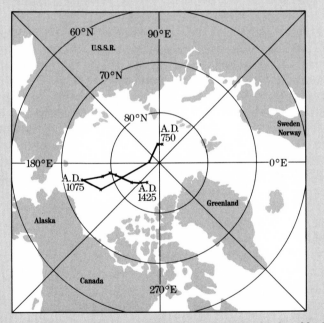

Adapted from a computer plot of the archaeomagnetic curve developed by Robert S. Sternberg, this map illustrates the path of the magnetic north pole between A.D. 750 and 1425.

possible to determine the approximate date when the hearth was used. This technique can determine the age of a hearth to within 50 years and has become an extremely important tool for dating Hohokam sites.

A series of steps, illustrated in the accompanying photographs, must be followed to obtain samples for archaeomagnetic dating. First, small blocks are carved out of the hearth; no less than six samples are taken from each hearth in a tedious and time-consuming process. Care must be taken so that there is no movement of the clay from its original position. Each block of clay is then fitted with an aluminum cube designed for this purpose. The cubes are then filled with a special non-magnetic plaster, encasing the block of clay inside the cube.

Helga Teiwes

Once the plaster has hardened, careful compass readings are taken of the exact position of each cube. The cubes are finally pried up and additional plaster is put on the bottom side, thus completely enclosing the clay sample in plaster. The sets of cubes from each hearth are then taken to the laboratory, where their magnetism is measured and the orientation of the magnetic particles determined. Their orientation is then matched with the curve showing the wanderings of the pole through past centuries, and an approximate date is obtained.

Over 150 such samples were taken from hearths at Las Colinas. They showed that the site was occupied for over 450 years—from about A.D. 900 or 950 through A.D. 1450.

recovered, the style of the houses, and other means of dating showed that the village was founded during the Sedentary period, at approximately A.D. 900 or 950; it was then continuously occupied until the end of the Classic period, at about A.D. 1450.

Over 150 Hohokam houses were unearthed, occurring in clusters of groups consisting of two to six houses each. These clusters are similar to those found at other Hohokam sites and probably represent a set of dwellings occupied by a family group. Not all of the houses were built or occupied simultaneously, however; nor were they all used as living space. By determining which houses *were* there at the same time, and by distinguishing the houses that were actually lived in from those used for storage or other special purposes, it is possible to estimate the population of the village at various times during the occupation. Based on the information recovered from the houses at Las Colinas, it has been estimated that a maximum of 200 to 250 people lived in this area of the village at any given time.

One of the most important aspects of Las Colinas was the presence of at least four platform mounds, only one of which was located within the freeway

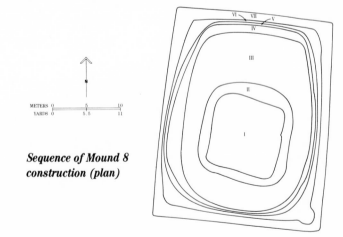

METERS 0   5   10
YARDS 0   5.5   11

Sequence of Mound 8 construction (plan)

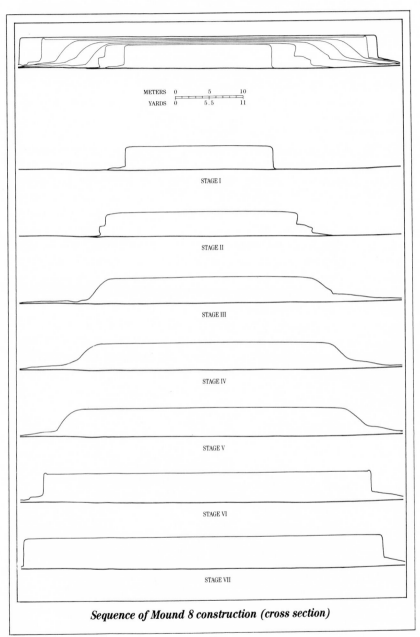

METERS 0   5   10
YARDS 0   5.5   11

STAGE I

STAGE II

STAGE III

STAGE IV

STAGE V

STAGE VI

STAGE VII

Sequence of Mound 8 construction (cross section)

corridor. Renewed excavations at Mound 8 showed that this mound was first constructed about the time the ballcourt was abandoned—around A.D. 1100—and that it had been enlarged six times. This sequence of construction provided a unique picture of the development of this kind of structure (see illustrations, pages 48 and 49). It was also discovered that the area of Mound 8 was always set off to the east from the major concentration of houses in the village, with very few houses or other features located in the intervening space. In addition, very large houses, different from those discovered elsewhere on the site, were arranged in formal patterns around the mound.

The first six stages of the mound were topped by a small, insubstantial structure, and it is unlikely that anyone actually lived there. During this time, the mound may have been a place where some sort of ritual took place. During the seventh stage, however, houses were constructed on top of the mound and used as dwellings, and a large wall was built, enclosing the mound and its associated houses. These changes signal an important shift in the function of the mound and may indicate that the people who lived there enjoyed a higher status than the rest of the villagers. Some idea of the size, and probably the importance, of Las Colinas may be gained by recalling that there were at least three other platform mounds at the site, all of them *larger* than Mound 8.

Some evidence indicates that not all of the people who lived at Las Colinas were Hohokam. One group of houses at the western edge of the site was apparently occupied by Patayan peoples whose homeland was in the lower reaches of the Gila River and in the adjoining Colorado River Valley (see map, page 20). Several of these houses were rebuilt or remodeled, suggesting that they stood for some time. The longevity of this house group, the abundance of Patayan pottery found in and around the houses, and a nearby cremation of a kind peculiar to the Patayan groups indicate that these non-Hohokam visitors actually lived at Las Colinas for as long as a generation or more. The presence of a Patayan group at Las Colinas cannot be explained at present. Perhaps they served as laborers, working on the Hohokam canals in exchange for foodstuffs or craft goods at a time when the Hohokam were expanding their irrigation systems. Perhaps intermarriage brought new Patayan relatives into the village for a time. Whatever the reasons, the discovery of evidence pointing to a Patayan presence at the site was an unexpected result of the investigations.

Pottery from the areas around Flagstaff showed that the villagers of Las Colinas also had contact with the Anasazi people of that region. This material was not nearly so abundant as the Patayan pottery, nor was it concentrated in a single area, indicating that it was not the product of people actually living at Las Colinas as the Patayan group did. Only particular types of vessels from the Anasazi area reached Las Colinas, further supporting the idea that this pottery was probably obtained on a limited basis through trade. The fact that Anasazi vessels were recovered from several cremation deposits at the site and have been recovered from cremations at other Hohokam sites, may suggest that they were highly valued items, because of their distinctive appearance and because of the long distance over which they had to travel to reach the Hohokam. Relationships with the Patayan and Anasazi groups were apparently the most important external contacts for the people of Las Colinas. Very little of the intrusive pottery recovered originated in the Mogollon area to the northeast, east, and south.

Many important discoveries were made at Las Colinas, and the results of these excavations will be examined and reexamined, discussed, and reinterpreted many times as these findings are integrated into the body of current knowledge about the Hohokam. Perhaps the most significant aspect of the excavations was that they provided a sample of a large village that was occupied throughout the Sedentary to Classic period transition, and thus produced a substantial body of information with which to assess this important and complex time of change in Hohokam prehistory.

The ultimate aim of an excavation is to draw together the very varied strands of evidence into a coherent whole. The detailed dissection of a site and the elaborate recording of all its observable phenomena are simply the preludes to an attempt to give meaning to the evidence.

Philip Barker

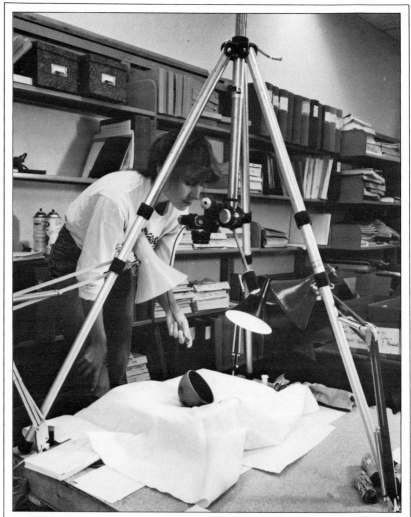

Laboratory workers sort, identify, count, and weigh the thousands of artifacts recovered from Las Colinas. Whole ceramic vessels, shell jewelry, and other diagnostic artifacts are individually numbered, cataloged, and photographed. The excavation of a site is only the first step in a long and involved process designed to obtain a variety of information about the lifeways of prehistoric peoples.

CHAPTER FOUR

A COMPLEX WEALTH OF INFORMATION

As is the case with any archaeological site, the excavation of Las Colinas was only one step in the long and complex process of retrieving the information contained in the remains. Over two years have been spent in the full analysis and interpretation of the materials recovered from the site, beginning with the washing, sorting, and labeling of artifacts. This basic processing was followed by more detailed recording of measurements and other characteristics of the artifacts recovered, as well as analyses of the spatial and temporal distributions of different types of features—houses, cremations, outdoor ovens, and so forth—using maps and field records. This information will be synthesized to produce a cohesive picture of the lives of the people of Las Colinas and to provide new insights into the ways they organized and conceived of their world. The results of these efforts will be published in a series of reports presenting both the data collected during excavation and analysis and the conclusions derived therefrom.

Each archaeological site contains many kinds of information that may be relevant to research problems of interest to the archaeologist. As noted above, the size of houses and their clustering into groups may tell how many people occupied the site and something of the kinds of social units in which they lived. Hearths or other burned features may produce samples that aid the archaeologist in determining how old the site is (see box, page 44). Artifacts such as pottery and stone tools show the ways in which foods were processed and stored, and the distributions of different types of tools may indicate areas within the village where certain tasks were performed. Pottery also helps place the remains in time, because certain decorative styles are associated with particular parts of the chronology. The volume of subterranean storage pits shows how much food could have been kept there, while the refuse produced in everyday activities and discarded in pits, in abandoned houses, or in surface deposits can tell the archaeologist much about the diet and food habits of the villagers (see box, page 58). The presence of structures such as ballcourts and platform mounds indicates important aspects of the social and religious life of the people, and the manner in which the deceased were treated (burial in special areas, the inclusion of exotic grave offerings) can reveal clues to different statuses that may have existed in the society. The health and longevity of the people, and the diseases and accidents they suffered, may be determined by examining the bones themselves. These are but a few examples of the kinds of information collected from archaeological sites and put together by the archaeologist in order to reconstruct the lifeways of prehistoric peoples.

The collection of information from an archaeological site does not proceed blindly, however, and preparation begins long before the first shovel of dirt is

turned. From the beginning of the excavation through the processing and analysis of the materials recovered, the archaeologist is guided by a *research design:* a document written before the excavation begins, outlining the kinds of problems and questions to be investigated. Decisions about what to excavate, what kinds of samples to take, and what kinds of analyses to apply to the materials recovered are made on the basis of the problems defined in the research design, and considerable time and effort are spent in preparing that document. During this process, the archaeologist tries to take into account the nature of the site or sites to be studied, as well as the gaps in existing archaeological knowledge that may be filled with the resulting information. Thus the research design provides organization and direction to the fieldwork and to the subsequent analyses.

Obviously not all questions may be answered in the course of a single project. The archaeologist cannot always predict what he will actually find in a given site and how that information may be important to issues that were *not* addressed in the research design. Because careful records are kept and the many notes, maps, artifacts, and samples are permanently stored, other researchers may subsequently reexamine these materials with different problems or questions in mind. The skill of the archaeologist and the meticulous

Lessons from Hohokam Trash

By examining the garbage of a modern household, much can be learned about the lives of the people who discarded the material. The same is true of prehistoric peoples, and the trash deposits found in Hohokam villages are one of the richest sources of information available to the archaeologist. The Hohokam dug holes in the ground to mine earth for house construction, clay for pottery making, and for other purposes; they often refilled these holes with the debris produced by everyday activities.

Abandoned house pits, roasting pits, and other such features were also often filled with trash. By carefully collecting and processing samples from these pits, and by analyzing the fragments of artifacts and debris contained in them, the details of everyday village life are revealed. These studies often involve specialists such as botanists and geologists, who identify the materials and aid the archaeologist in reconstructing the lifeways of the prehistoric people.

Many pits like this one, filled with the refuse of everyday life, were excavated at Las Colinas.

Pottery from far-off northern Arizona was probably obtained through trade, demonstrating that the world of the Hohokam was not restricted to the desert valleys.

Fragments of charred plants show that the villagers of Las Colinas grew corn, beans, squash, and cotton and that they collected and ate a variety of wild plants as well.

Animal bones indicate that the villagers most often hunted and ate small mammals, particularly rabbits. Larger animals such as deer were only occasional additions to their diet.

recording of observations made during the excavations largely determine the value of the collections and the success of those later investigations. Although the site cannot be reexcavated, these documents should provide a clear picture of the site as it was.

A number of basic field methods are used by the archaeologist during the excavation of a site, to insure that the information will be collected systematically and in a way that will facilitate subsequent analyses. A numbered *grid system* is established over the site so that the location of any feature or artifact discovered may be precisely plotted in horizontal space; similarly, a *vertical datum* for the site is established, so that the depth of features and deposits may be consistently recorded. Thus the position within this system of every house, pit, burial, or other feature is recorded, and each of these features is given its own set of numbers, referred to as its *provenience*. Every bag of material collected is labeled, and the provenience information is not only included on all notes and maps but even appears in the photographs taken during the excavations. In this way, the artifacts and samples collected from any specific location within the site are distinguished from those that come from other proveniences. Later, in the laboratory, these same numbers are used in the computerization of information, so that the various analyses may be more easily and quickly performed.

Just as great care is taken during the excavations to insure that all materials are collected and recorded properly, so must time and care be taken during the analysis of those materials. Results are checked and rechecked to confirm the conclusions reached. Often unexpected results occur, and the archaeologist must be certain that these are correctly interpreted (see box, page 59). In order to complete the analysis and interpretation of excavated materials, the aid of specialists is often enlisted. These people may be archaeologists with special skills or scientists trained in other disciplines, and they make an extremely important contribution to our understanding of the lifeways of prehistoric peoples. *Botanists* identify seeds and fragments of plants, and *palynologists* identify the pollen grains produced by plants, to aid in the reconstruction of the prehistoric environment and to provide information about the crops that were grown, the wild foods that were collected, and

The Reservoirs That Weren't

On the western edge of the village, two large basins were discovered, each measuring over 15 meters (about 50 feet) in diameter and over 3 meters (about 10 feet) deep. A combination of factors—a canal that emptied into one of the basins and the presence of water-laid sediments in both basins—suggested that these features were reservoirs where the people of the village stored water for everyday use. Such reservoirs have been found at other Hohokam villages, and the basins at Las Colinas appeared to be two more examples of this type of water-storage feature.

Large blocks of the basins were excavated, soil samples were taken for later analysis, and the complex layers of sediments were carefully described and recorded. These studies indicated that the villagers had dug out each basin several times, after which it again filled with water. Large drying cracks in the sediments showed that the basins had been dry much of the time. What good was a reservoir that did not hold water very often? Back in the laboratory, analysis of the pollen samples from the basins confirmed that they had

A profile of one of the large basins, showing the complex layering of water-laid sediments. Careful documentation and detailed analyses showed that the basins held water only for brief periods.

indeed been dry most of the time, as determined by the kinds of plants that grew in and around them. Closer examination of the layers revealed that the basins were dug out *each time a large deposit of pure clay had accumulated,* leading to the solution of the puzzle: the basins were designed to collect clay—probably for pottery making—rather than to hold water for everyday use.

therefore about the prehistoric diet. *Zooarchaeologists* identify animal bones found in sites, contributing additional information about the prehistoric environment and the dietary habits of the people. *Physical anthropologists* examine the human remains recovered, identifying the age and sex of the individuals represented and describing observed pathologies. These are abnormalities caused by factors such as disease, poor diet, and injury that may be apparent on the bones. *Geologists* or *geomorphologists* may be called upon to identify the rocks and minerals that were used to make tools or for other purposes, and may also aid in the recording and interpretation of the complex layerings or stratigraphy of deposits within the sites. The geomorphologist is particularly important in helping the archaeologist understand the design and functioning of canal systems. *Chemists* and *physicists* may perform detailed technical analyses that can answer a variety of questions, such as the composition of clays used to make pottery and the natural sources from which those clays may have come. These and many other specialists add important dimensions to the information that may be gained from archaeological sites.

Not all sites are as large or as productive as Las Colinas, but all contain information that can be used to understand the ways of life followed by prehistoric peoples. The archaeologist must not only recover and analyze the material, but interpret it carefully and completely as well, correlating the results of individual analyses into a cohesive whole that addresses the questions identified in the research design. In these time-consuming and tedious tasks, he calls upon all of his skills and those of other experts to insure that the maximum amount of information is gleaned from the bits and pieces of the past.

Our ideals, laws, and
customs should be based on
the proposition that each
generation in turn becomes
the custodian rather than
the absolute owner of our
resources—
and each generation has
the obligation to
pass this inheritance on to
the future.

Alden Whitman

The visitors' center at Las Colinas, with its interpretive displays, attracted many interested citizens. Staff members also conducted tours of the excavations in progress for school groups and other organizations.

CHAPTER FIVE

ARCHAEOLOGY AND THE PUBLIC

In addition to producing a wealth of scientific information, the excavations at Las Colinas gave the general public a unique opportunity to visit an archaeological excavation in progress. A visitors' center was set up on the site, with interpretive displays explaining Hohokam culture and showing how archaeologists work. Scheduled tours of the site were given three times a week, with staff members available to answer questions. Numerous school classes from the Phoenix area visited the site, as did senior citizens and other groups. Members of the Arizona Archaeological Society, a group of amateur archaeologists, excavated at the site on weekends under the supervision of project staff members who volunteered their time. Over 3,000 people came to see Las Colinas while it was being excavated, and many came away with a better understanding of the achievements of the Hohokam and an appreciation of the work done by archaeologists. Through such programs, the public is made aware of the need for a concern for cultural resources and of the kinds of information archaeologists are able to recover about past societies through systematic study.

Public interest in and concern for archaeological remains has a long history in the United States. Thomas Jefferson, an avid amateur archaeologist, recorded information about prehistoric mounds in the eastern United States that is still used today. Some of the early settlers of the Phoenix area were intrigued by the prehistoric remains they found there and the notes and maps made by those observers are valuable records of the appearance of those sites—including Las Colinas—prior to modern development. Today, this interest in our

Governmental Protection o

FEDERAL

Antiquities Act of 1906

Provided for government protection of any object of antiquity on federal lands; empowered President to reserve as national monuments public lands having historic, prehistoric, or scientific significance.

Historic Sites Act of 1935

Called for inventory and in-place preservation of properties of national historic or archaeological significance, for the designation and acquisition of national historical landmarks, and for intergovernmental and interdisciplinary efforts in historic preservation.

Reservoir Salvage Act of 1960

Required that any agency of the United States government inform the Secretary of the Interior of plans for the construction of any federally funded, licensed, or sponsored dam. Required archaeological survey in such cases and made the Secretary responsible for implementing any further research.

National Historic Preservation Act of 1966

Provided for an expanded National Register of districts, sites, buildings, structures, and objects significant to American history, architecture, archaeology, and culture by providing matching funds to conduct state-wide surveys for their location. Also established the Advisory Council on Historic Preservation, which drafts guidelines for implementing National Register programs and assists state and local governments in drafting historic preservation legislation.

National Environmental Policy Act of 1969

Directs all agencies of the Federal Government to identify and develop methods that will insure that unquantified environmental amenities and values are given consideration in decision-making procedures. Also called for the preparation of an environmental impact statement on any major federal action that significantly affects the environment.

Executive Order No. 11,593

Issued by the President in 1971, this document expanded upon the Na-

ur Cultural Resources

tional Historic Preservation Act of 1966 and the National Environmental Policy Act of 1969. It mandates that all Executive Branch agencies, bureaus, and offices: (1) compile an inventory of the cultural resources of which they are trustee, (2) nominate all eligible government properties to the National Register of Historic Places, (3) preserve and protect their cultural resources, and (4) insure that agency activities aid in preserving and protecting of non-federally owned cultural resources.

Archaeological and Preservation Act of 1974

This act amended the Reservoir Salvage Act of 1960, explicitly requiring all federal agencies to conduct appropriate archaeological investigations prior to undertaking any project that might result in the destruction of significant remains and authorized federal agencies to use their own funds for archaeological investigations.

Archaeological Resources Protection Act of 1979

Enacted to strengthen control over vandalism of sites, especially as a result of unauthorized excavations motivated by high prices paid for prehistoric North American art. It sets forth definitions of protected cultural resources and penalties for violators.

1980 Amendments to the National Historic Preservation Act of 1966

These amendments made the provisions of Executive Order 11,593 a part of the NHPA statute.

STATE

Arizona Antiquities Act of 1981

Amended and strengthened in recent years, this act defines "archaeological specimens," states who qualifies for an excavation permit, and how that person or agency must treat archaeological resources. Also details felony penalties in the form of fines and prison terms for those convicted of breaking this law.

Historic Preservation Act of 1983

Establishes a historic preservation policy for Arizona, requires stewardship responsibility for state owned or controlled properties, institutionalizes a state historic preservation program, and defines conditions under which owners of historic homes may receive tax reductions.

nation's past is expressed in a variety of ways. The number of people who visit state and national parks and monuments featuring historic and prehistoric sites increases annually. Amateur archaeological groups and local historical societies are found throughout the country, and many of them sponsor active and well-attended programs. The information taught in classrooms through books and films, as well as that used to develop museum displays, results ultimately from archaeological research. It is a long way from the detailed technical investigation of an archaeological site to the museum display and the classroom film, but, without archaeological research, neither would be possible. Education about cultural resources is important; archaeologists have a responsibility to share the results of their efforts with the interested public. In turn, a well-informed public, in addition to satisfying its curiosity about the archaeology of the region, is better able to appreciate the need for preservation of archaeological sites or, alternatively, for data recovery at the sites that must be destroyed in the course of modern development. Public programs such as the one conducted at Las Colinas provide a tangible return on the tax dollars spent on archaeology by federal, state, and local agencies.

As early as 1906, federal legislation provided for the protection of archaeological resources and for the establishment of national monuments on public lands having historic, prehistoric, or scientific significance. More recently, laws insuring the appropriate treatment of cultural resources have been enacted at both state and federal levels in response to the dramatic increase in the rate of destruction of cultural and natural resources which accompanied the rapid economic growth of the 1950s and 1960s (see box, page 66). It was under the provisions of such legislation that the work at Las Colinas was accomplished.

The laws which protect cultural resources are important not only in providing guidelines for the proper treatment of these remains but also in establishing severe penalties for those who would selfishly destroy valuable sites for personal gain or recreation. Every year, thousands of archaeological sites are badly disturbed or destroyed by "pot hunters," vandals who dig indiscriminately for artifacts to sell or simply to satisfy their own curiosity. Existing laws provide for the punishment of those who ignore the fact that these resources belong to everyone; proper education can insure that there will be fewer of these people in the future.

As we sort through the technical complexities of archaeological research, the people of Las Colinas come through the counts and weights and maps and notes. We are struck by their remarkable canal systems, by the beauty of their pottery, shell jewelry, and of the other artifacts they fashioned, and by the energy and industry they put into building their homes, ballcourts, and platform mounds. This is the intangible attraction of the past that can fire the imagination of even the most experienced archaeologist as well as that of the general public. Exposure to the remains of Las Colinas and to other such sites brings us into contact with the births, lives, and deaths of the generations of people who lived there. We can imagine a work party struggling to repair a canal damaged by a flood. We can envision women working in front of mud-walled houses, preparing food or mending baskets while children play nearby and dogs scavenge trash dumps for bits of food. We can see the smoke from many fires rising to form a haze above the valley where the skyline is now dominated by the steel and concrete of the twentieth century.

Archaeological research provides the stuff of these visions, projections that create curiosity and wonder about the prehistoric people as well as an identification with their basic humanity. And, by the very fact of their antiquity, the remains they have left create a sense of time that extends far beyond our brief and narrow existence. Fostered by an expanded sense of time, a sense of responsibility comes from the realization of the fragile and impermanent nature of our own lives. Just as the decisions made by the Hohokam affected the course of their society over the centuries, so decisions made now will affect the ability of future generations to survive and will determine the quality of life that those generations experience. An obligation to future generations will be fulfilled and the potential quality of life enhanced by current and future efforts to insure the protection, preservation, and appropriate scientific study of our many cultural resources. To the degree that the study of the past can help foster this long-term view of our own lives, of our debt to past generations, and our obligations to future ones, archaeology goes beyond satisfying parochial curiosities and has real and lasting lessons to teach.

SUGGESTED READINGS

For those interested in learning more about archaeology and the Hohokam, the following books and articles are recommended.

Doyel, David E.
1979   The prehistoric Hohokam of the Arizona desert. *American Scientist* 67(5): 544-54.

Gregonis, Linda M., and Karl J. Reinhard
1979   *Hohokam Indians of the Tucson Basin.* Tucson: University of Arizona Press.

Haury, Emil W.
1967   The Hohokam, first masters of the American desert. *National Geographic* 131(5): 670-95.

1976   *The Hohokam: Desert Farmers and Craftsmen.* Tucson: University of Arizona Press.

Turney, Omar A.
1929   *Prehistoric Irrigation in Arizona.* Phoenix: Arizona State Historian.

Weaver, Kenneth F.
1967   Magnetic clues help date the past. *National Geographic* 131(5): 696-701.

A seven-volume report covering the recent excavations at Las Colinas, *Arizona State Museum Archaeological Series* 162, is available from the Cultural Resource Management Division, Arizona State Museum, University of Arizona.

About the Authors

Michael H. Bartlett received a B.A. in Anthropology from the University of Arizona in 1977, and has participated in archaeological fieldwork in Arizona, New Mexico, and Colorado. Bartlett has served as the Public Programs Supervisor for the Las Colinas Project and as an archaeologist with the Tucson office of New World Research, Inc.

Thomas M. Kolaz received a B.A. in Anthropology in 1977 and a Master of Education in Museum Education in 1982 from the University of Arizona. Kolaz has worked for several private and state museums, and for the National Park Service. He served as the Assistant Public Programs Supervisor for the Las Colinas Project and subsequently as the Director of Public Programs for the Institute for American Research, Tucson Division.

David A. Gregory received a B.S. in Anthropology from Wisconsin State University (Oshkosh) in 1970 and an M.A. in Anthropology from the University of Arizona in 1972. He has participated in archaeological research in Wisconsin, Arizona, and Yucatan, and has worked for the Cultural Resource Management Division of the Arizona State Museum. Gregory was the Director of the Las Colinas Project.